BALANCING HOME & CAREER:

Skills For Successful Life Management

Third Edition

Pamela J. Conrad

A FIFTY-MINUTE™ SERIES BOOK

CRISP PUBLICATIONS, INC.
Menlo Park, California

BALANCING HOME & CAREER:
Skills For Successful Life Management
Third Edition

Pamela J. Conrad

CREDITS:
Editor: **Michael Crisp**
Composition and Layout: **Interface Studio**
Cover Design: **Carol Harris**
Illustrations: **Ralph Mapson**

Copyright © 1986, 1990, 1995 by Crisp Publications, Inc.
Printed in the United States of America

http://www.crisp-pub.com

Distribution to the U.S. Trade:

National Book Network, Inc.
4720 Boston Way
Lanham, MD 20706
1-800-462-6420

Library of Congress Catalog Card Number 89-81910
Conrad, Pamela J.
Balancing Home and Career
ISBN 1-56052-355-7

This book is printed on recyclable paper with soy ink.

LEARNING OBJECTIVES FOR:

BALANCING HOME AND CAREER

The objectives for *Balancing Home and Career* are listed below. They have been developed to guide you, the reader, to the core issues covered in this book.

Objectives

❏ **1) To explain the skills needed to manage home and business activities.**

❏ **2) To provide experience solving case studies.**

❏ **3) To present overall strategies for successful life management.**

Assessing Your Progress

In addition to the Learning Objectives, Crisp, Inc. has developed an **assessment** that covers the fundamental information presented in this book. A twenty-five item, multiple choice/true-false questionnaire allows the reader to evaluate his or her comprehension of the subject matter. An answer sheet with a summary matching the questions to the listed objectives is also available. To learn how to obtain a copy of this assessment please call: **1-800-442-7477** and ask to speak with a Customer Service Representative.

ABOUT THE AUTHOR

With experience in balancing a home and career of over 30 years of parenting and 23 years in a corporate career, Pamela Conrad is able to share her learning as a pre-school teacher, identifying the needs of working parents, and later as a Vice President in banking as Training Director in the credit card industry. Born and raised in Los Angeles, a DePaul University graduate, she currently resides in the Chicago area with her husband and her two 83 year old in-laws; and she is *still* balancing a home and career.

ABOUT THE SERIES

With over 200 titles in print, the acclaimed Crisp 50-Minute™ series presents self-paced learning at its easiest and best. These comprehensive self-study books for business or personal use are filled with exercises, activities, assessments, and case studies that capture your interest and increase your understanding.

Other Crisp products, based on the 50-Minute books, are available in a variety of learning style formats for both individual and group study, including audio, video, CD-ROM, and computer-based training.

CONTENTS

CONTENTS (Continued)

INTRODUCTION:
WHAT ARE YOU JUGGLING?

Check items which involve you in each category:

HOME	CAREER	RECREATION	COMMUNITY INVOLVEMENT
_____ Mate	_____ School/Class	_____ Tennis	_____ Church
_____ Parent(s)	_____ Work at Home	_____ Golf	_____ Charity
_____ Child(ren)	_____ Own A Business	_____ Cycling	_____ Professional Organization
_____ Pet(s)	_____ Work for others	_____ Exercise	_____ Community
_____ Housekeeping	_____ Manage others	_____ Jogging	_____ Youth Group
_____ Laundry	_____ Deadlines	_____ Boating	_____ School
_____ Yardwork	_____ Commute	_____ Dancing	_____ Social Group
_____ Bill paying	_____ Accountabilities	_____ Other sport	_____ Health Club
_____ Shopping	_____ Budget	_____ TV	_____ Chamber of Commerce
_____ Meal preparation	_____ Demanding Boss	_____ Entertaining	_____ Political group
_____ Auto maintenance	_____ Pressure	_____ Spectator sports	_____ Others
_____ Play	_____ Travel	_____ Hobby	_____ Homeowners Ass'n
_____ Others	_____ Others	_____ Others	_____ Ethic Group
_____ Others	_____ Others	_____ Others	_____ Others
_____ TOTAL	_____ TOTAL	_____ TOTAL	_____ TOTAL

> *If you have a column without any checkmarks—consider if you have balance in your life. If you have checked at least one in each column you appear to have some variety in your life. Too many checks in any column may suggest some imbalance.

IF YOU'RE LIKE MOST PEOPLE . . .

- You're involved in many things which create a more complicated lifestyle than your parents and grandparents experienced.

- You enjoy taking advantage of new opportunities even though they make life more complex.

This book will help you sort through the challenges you have to deal with now; the opportunities you want to explore; and steps you need to take to bring balance to your life.

A DEFINITION OF BALANCE:

> *To regulate and keep in a state of just proportion*
> Webster

Some believe that it is easier to balance home and career when leisure time becomes a third element. The claim is made that the responsibilities of both a career and a home can put you on "overload," and a third element is needed as a safety zone.

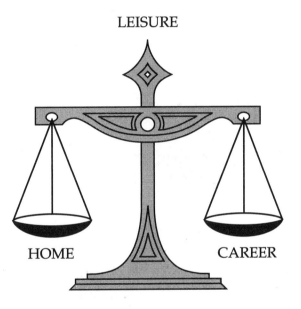

This third factor is private time. It is the stabilizing element that pulls us away from our responsibilities and allows us to do something for ourselves. Most professional counselors advocate at least three hours a week for personal relaxation and recreation. Private time can be involvement in the arts, additional education, or some form of exercise.

Private time can help if you feel you are focusing only on the responsibilities of a home and career. Before it becomes self-defeating, find some time just for "you". Without some leisure time, it is impossible to see either home or career in true perspective.

A working spouse needs space to do his or her own thing, away from the other—especially when children are involved. Unless this is honored by both, balance for either spouse may be impossible to achieve.

SET SOME OBJECTIVES

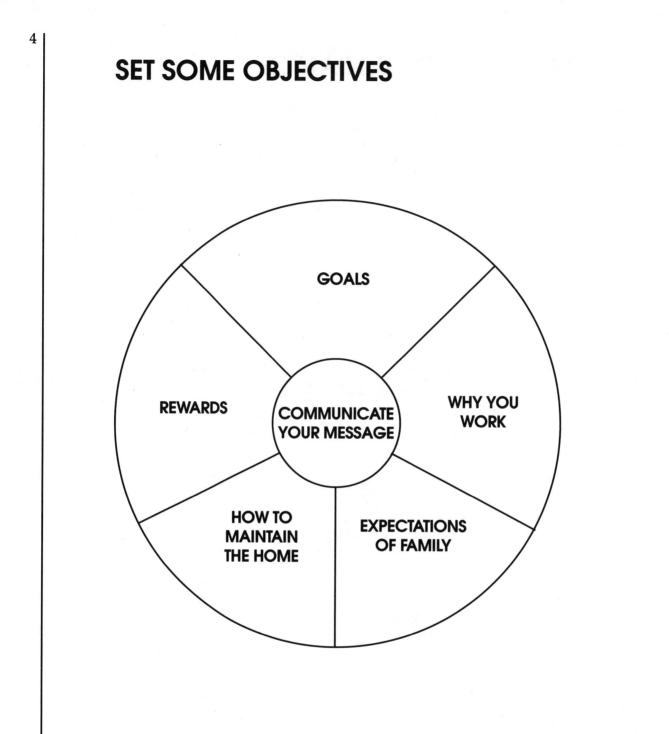

ESTABLISHING YOUR GOALS

Many successful individuals claim you can be anything you want to be; have anything you want and do anything you choose; providing you set some goals and prioritize the necessary steps to achieve them.

When you want something badly enough, it's usually worth your time and effort. List your goals below even if they seem unreachable.

My most important CAREER goal (status, a new job, recognition, etc.)

In one year _____

In three years _____

In five years _____

My most important HOME goal (family, financial, organization, etc.)

In one year _____

In three years _____

In five years _____

My most important LEISURE goal (personal, family, recreational.)

In one year _____

In three years _____

In five years _____

As you establish goals, give yourself permission to be outstanding, and have some fun. Then, communicate your goals to anyone you want to be part of your support system.

P.S. You have just completed the first step in reaching your goals.

6

THE REWARD OF A THING
WELL DONE, IS TO HAVE
DONE IT.

Emerson

PRIORITIZE THE BENEFITS OF WORKING

Rank from 1 to 14. 1 being most important, 14 being least important.

I WORK FOR:

_____   Self-gratification

_____   Freedom/independence

_____   Excitement

_____   Money

_____   Recognition

_____   Experience

_____   Health care and benefits

_____   The opportunity to meet people

_____   Achievement

_____   Challenge

_____   Status/title

_____   Security

_____   Self-esteem

_____   _____
            (add your own)

All are valid reasons for working, however, the bottom line is:

WE WORK BECAUSE WE NEED TO insure that we have food, shelter and clothing. Discussing the benefits of working with family, friends and co-workers helps you maintain a more positive attitude toward your job.

Perhaps you were surprised if money was not the most important reason you work. Once you have satisfied the basic needs (food, shelter and clothing), other human needs become important.

PRIORITIZE YOUR RESPONSIBILITIES AT HOME

Rank from 1 to 15. 1 being most important, 15 being least important.

_____ Interaction with family members

_____ Housekeeping

_____ Meal preparation

_____ Grocery shopping

_____ Child care (development/maintenance)

_____ Laundry

_____ Yardwork/gardening

_____ Pet care

_____ Youth activities

_____ Decorating

_____ Maintenance and repairs (home, auto, etc.)

_____ Entertaining

_____ Quiet time

_____ Relationships with neighbors

_____ Bill paying

_____ _____
                (add your own)

Everyone has responsibilities at home. Some participate only when asked. Others carry an imbalance of responsibility.

It is critical to communicate your expectations to keep home activities running smoothly. Any time one individual feels burdened with too much home responsibility, it is usually because the priorities have not been discussed. Conflict may be the result. Communicate your expectations of how your home might be managed with whomever you live with. Be flexible when agreeing to the distribution of responsibilities and try to achieve a balance.

What you do to free your mind from career pressures and home demands often provides temporary escape in which to relax and unwind. Those who do not allow enough "time out" in their lives often experience the physical or mental affects of stored up stress. List those leisure activities you enjoy or would like to explore, that will improve your "time out."

EXPLORE YOUR LEISURE TIME

PRIORITIZE YOUR LEISURE ACTIVITIES

Include hobbies or involvements you would like to experience as well as those in which you are currently engaged. Rank activities from 1 to 14, with 1 being your favorite, and 14 being your least favorite way to spend leisure time.

_____ Organized sports

_____ Entertaining

_____ Hobbies

_____ Shopping

_____ Theatre, Symphony or Ballet

_____ Camping

_____ Reading

_____ Travel

_____ Church or charity

_____ Watching television

_____ Exercise

_____ Community or political involvement

_____ Family outings

_____ _____
(add your own)

Research shows that "workaholics" may be less productive than those who take leisure time. Time away from career and home responsibilities can refresh your spirit and make you more efficient. Leisure time is a necessity, not a luxury.

WHO BENEFITS
WHEN YOU WORK?

Most people work because economically it is necessary. However, when you complete the following questions you may find some benefits beyond the necessities of life.

1. How does your significant other (spouse, boyfriend, girlfriend) benefit from your working?

   _____

   _____

   _____

2. How do your children (if any), benefit when you work?

   _____

   _____

   _____

3. How does your employer benefit?

   _____

   _____

   _____

4. How do you benefit? (What do you gain besides a paycheck?)

   _____

   _____

   _____

5. Does anyone else benefit because you work?

   _____

   _____

   _____

Do those who benefit by your working understand what their benefits are? Adults often take the benefits of working for granted. Children usually don't recognize the rewards working parents provide. Discuss the benefits of working with your family and friends. Communicate!

BALANCE SCALE

How you feel about your current situation is important. It determines the energy you give to career, family, home environment, physical needs and perhaps most important the things you enjoy. To measure the degree of balance in your life, complete this exercise.

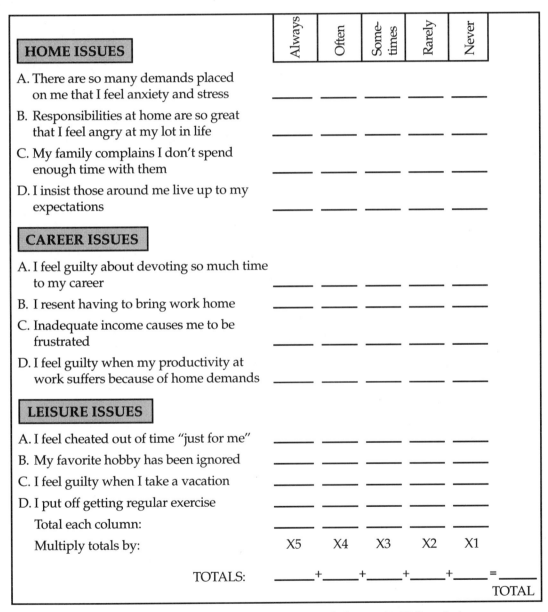

	Always	Often	Some-times	Rarely	Never
HOME ISSUES					
A. There are so many demands placed on me that I feel anxiety and stress	____	____	____	____	____
B. Responsibilities at home are so great that I feel angry at my lot in life	____	____	____	____	____
C. My family complains I don't spend enough time with them	____	____	____	____	____
D. I insist those around me live up to my expectations	____	____	____	____	____
CAREER ISSUES					
A. I feel guilty about devoting so much time to my career	____	____	____	____	____
B. I resent having to bring work home	____	____	____	____	____
C. Inadequate income causes me to be frustrated	____	____	____	____	____
D. I feel guilty when my productivity at work suffers because of home demands	____	____	____	____	____
LEISURE ISSUES					
A. I feel cheated out of time "just for me"	____	____	____	____	____
B. My favorite hobby has been ignored	____	____	____	____	____
C. I feel guilty when I take a vacation	____	____	____	____	____
D. I put off getting regular exercise	____	____	____	____	____
Total each column:	____	____	____	____	____
Multiply totals by:	X5	X4	X3	X2	X1

TOTALS: ____ + ____ + ____ + ____ + ____ = ____ TOTAL

10–20 Excellent balance, 21–30 Good balance, 31–40 Fair balance, 41–50 Poor balance

NOTE: Examine each category of issues. If you selected "always" or "often" consistently in any one category, perhaps that area needs attention to bring better balance into your life.

BALANCING YOUR LIFE IS A CONSTANT CHALLENGE

PRESCRIPTION FOR BALANCE

When the homefront is in balance you perform better at work

+

When your career is managed effectively, you're happier at home

+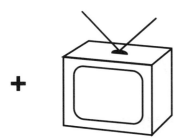

When there is a fair amount of leisure activity in your week, you feel revitalized and your life is enriched

= BALANCE

HOMEFRONT:
BALANCE BEGINS HERE

For most, HOME is the steady center of life. It is the comfort zone where we return for refueling, emotional support and privacy. Home is the place to disengage from structure and authority. It is a focal point to bring balance into your life.

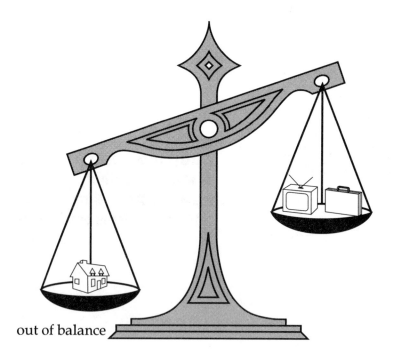

out of balance

CASE #1: DEBBIE'S DILEMMA

(SINGLE PARENT)

> As you read the following situation, think about steps you would recommend to help resolve Debbie's dilemma.

Debbie is a single parent who lives with her children. She works in a doctor's office and enjoys the contact with people. Her son, John, age ten, stays with a neighbor both before and after school. Jennifer, her daughter, age five, goes to a day care center.

Debbie's daily responsibility often seems overwhelming. Each morning she prepares breakfast, fixes bag lunches and organizes things she and the children need to take for the day. Debbie insists her children make their beds before leaving in the morning. Neither child however, is able to meet her standards, so she usually remakes the beds while they are eating. The children watch television and usually are not ready to leave when they should be. Debbie has been late to work several times during the last few months.

Debbie feels guilty for not being more a part of her children's day. John's teacher recently sent a note home that expressed concern about his behavior.

Debbie is often too tired to give the children much attention during the evening. There is dinner to decide upon and prepare, laundry to do, and John's homework to check. Also once a week it is Debbie's turn to bake cookies for the day care center's afternoon snack. Most evenings, all Debbie really wants to do is have a glass of wine and relax.

During her childhood, Debbie's mother devoted all of her time to homemaking. Debbie resents her role as a single parent. She projects her unhappiness to people she meets. Tardiness and stress are affecting her performance at work and she has been told that unless things improve, she will be terminated. She likes her job and the money meets her needs, but she feels trapped by her responsibilities at home and the expectations at work.

What steps do you recommend Debbie take?

See author's suggestions on page 83.

KEEPING THE HOMEFRONT POSITIVE

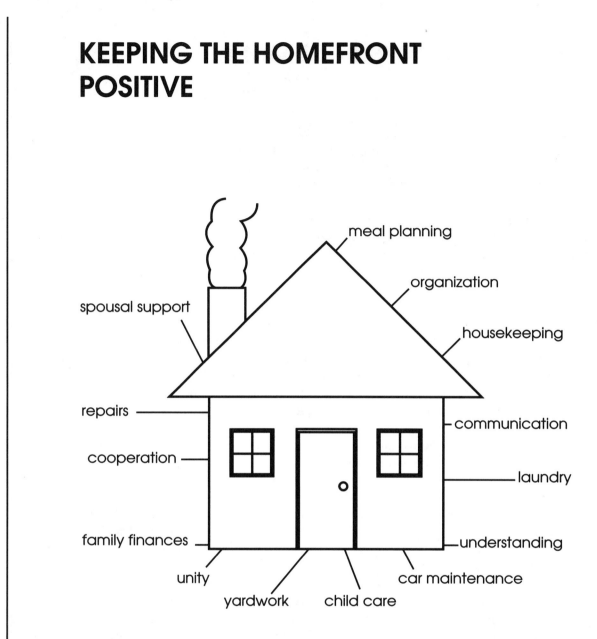

Running a home is complex. Fulfilling the expectations of each family member is difficult.

Complete the exercise on the facing page to identify the areas that require attention in your home.

HOMEFRONT EXPECTATIONS

| Check the homefront activities that others expect from you: |

_____ Time alone with family members   _____ Personal hygiene

_____ Parent/teacher relationships   _____ Empty trash

_____ Meal planning   _____ Yardwork

_____ Time with spouse/roommate   _____ Housecleaning

_____ Grocery shopping   _____ Laundry/cleaners

_____ Meal preparation   _____ Car pooling

_____ Dishes   _____ Car maintenance & repairs

_____ Helping with homework   _____ Making beds

_____ Errands   _____ Phone calls

_____ Medical visits   _____ Home repairs

_____ School support   _____ Pet needs

_____ Bringing in firewood   _____ Bookkeeping/bill paying

_____ Bathing children

_____   _____

(add your own)

Now cross out issues that have been discussed with others who share in the activity, or are under control.

| If you don't let people know what is expected they often disappoint you.

When you communicate expectations to others, you will probably feel more content with the way home activities are running. |

HOW WELL DO YOU KNOW . . . YOUR EXPECTATIONS???

Unless you find out they can become a stumbling block in your balancing act. Your expectations of others in the home must be discussed and agreed upon. They must be realistic. Discussing your expectations with others who could share homefront activities will usually result in an agreement to share responsibilities.

P.S.   Do you know what expectations family members have from you?

IDENTIFY THE EXPECTATION BARRIERS

Answer the following questions by circling YES or NO:

	YOU	FAMILY
1. Have you communicated your expectations of others in a positive way regarding the homefront issues that need attention:	YES NO	
Have family members communicated back?		YES NO
2. Can you identify how you benefit when everyone's expectations are being met?	YES NO	
Can family members explain how they benefit?		YES NO
3. Do you feel that some action is necessary to implement a more positive environment?	YES NO	
Do family members agree?		YES NO
4. Are you willing to contribute whatever is needed to support unity?	YES NO	
Are others in the home willing to do the same?		YES NO
5. Are you willing to allow others in your home to share the planning and organizing of activities?	YES NO	
Are the others willing to listen to your ideas?		YES NO
6. Are you prepared to exercise patience, and provide guidance while others learn to handle new home responsibilities?	YES NO	
Are family members equally prepared?		YES NO

If you answered NO to any question in the YOU column, think about how it affects your stress level. Consider whether your stress affects the homefront and then communicate any planned positive changes to your family.

If there is a NO in the family column, you will know where a barrier exists. The best approach is to communicate your feelings regularly and remain positive.

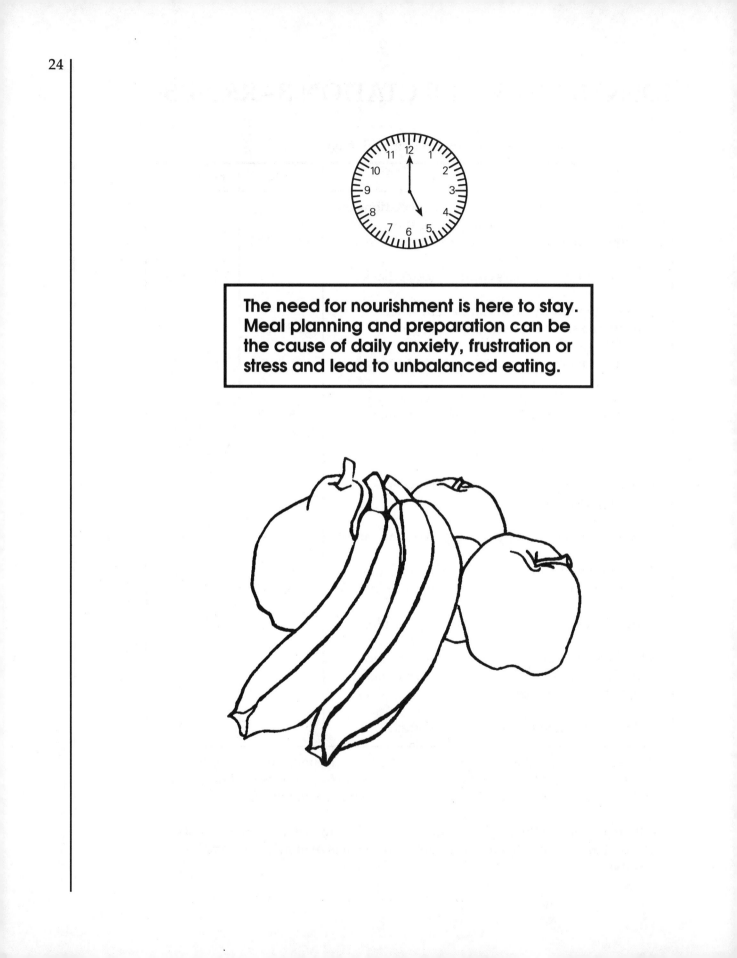

The need for nourishment is here to stay. Meal planning and preparation can be the cause of daily anxiety, frustration or stress and lead to unbalanced eating.

TIME SAVING TIPS AT HOME

Check the box ☑ if the ideas described will save you time and improve your eating habits.

☐ COMMUNICATING

1. Post a weekly menu that tells what is planned for dinner each night of the week. This will save having to make a decision each morning. By planning (and shopping ahead), all you need to do is defrost according to plan. Family members, (old enough to read), can assist by making salad or putting potatoes in the oven. Also members can be given regular duties like setting or cleaning the table. Be flexible with your menu. If you feel the need to change plans for an evening—DO IT!

2. Provide a central place for family members to list what they need the next time shopping is done. This helps put responsibility on the individual. Train the family to list items when they see the supply is running low. You should save planning time and fewer items will be forgotten during shopping trips.

     Cut here to make copies

- -

SUNDAY   SHOPPING LIST

_____

MONDAY

_____

TUESDAY

_____

WEDNESDAY

_____

THURSDAY

_____

FRIDAY

_____

SATURDAY

_____

TIME SAVING TIPS (Continued)

☐ FIX AHEAD FOOD
GIVE YOURSELF A NIGHT OFF!!!

Step 1   Prepare a double recipe or two casseroles instead of one
Step 2   Freeze for next week in an oven or microwave dish
Step 3   Cover with foil (for oven cooking), or plastic wrap (for microwave)
Step 4   Label with permanent marker: cooking time, temperature, covered or
         uncovered

Anyone who finds this dish on the kitchen sink can assist in the evening meal by
following the directions.

MAIN DISHES worth freezing

Taco Bake
1 lb hamburger
1 onion chopped
1 can diced green chiles
1 can tomato sauce
1 pkg. Taco Seasoning
1 tube Flaky biscuits
1 C Jack or Cheddar Cheese (grated)

Prepare Taco mix according to directions on package. Add chiles, and simmer while preparing dough. Separate biscuit dough into thin layers and line a 7 x 11 baking dish with half the dough. Sprinkle with $\frac{1}{2}$ C cheese. Spoon Taco mixture over the cheese. Top with remaining biscuits and cheese. Bake 30 min. 350°.

Beef Stroganoff
2 lbs round steak (sliced thin)
1 C chopped onion
1 can Beef Consomme
2 Tbls. Worstershire Sauce
12–15 mushrooms sliced
1 C Sour Cream
1 can Cream of Mushroom soup
2 Tbls. Catsup
1 pkg. wide noodles

In skillet brown meat and onions in oil. Add Consomme and Worstershire, simmer 45 min. Add water or wine if liquid boils away. Add remaining ingredients on low heat. Boil noodles, drain, spread in a glass dish, cover with Stroganoff. Cover and freeze for re-heating.

Burger-Rice Casserole
2 lbs hamburger
1 onion—chopped
1 C celery—chopped
1 clove garlic—crushed
1–48 oz. can V8 juice
1 tsp each: sugar, basil, oregano, parsley, salt, pepper, bay leaf
$1\frac{1}{2}$ C raw rice

LOW FAT

Shape meat into a large patty and saute 5 min. on each side. Cut into pieces in a casserole. Put all ingredients except rice in skillet and heat until boiling. Sprinkle rice over meat, add boiling liquid, cover and bake 45 min. at 350°, or until rice is tender and liquid is absorbed. Freeze.

Viva-La-Chicken
1 whole chicken
1 dozen Tortillas—torn in pieces
1 can Cream of Chicken soup
1 can Cream of Mushroom soup
1 C Milk
1 can Salsa (8 oz.)
1 onion—chopped
1 lb Cheddar Cheese—grated

Split chicken, bake 1 hr. at 350° or microwave 20 min. each side. Cool and remove meat from bones. Dice meat. Combine soups, milk, salsa and inion. In pyrex dish layer $\frac{1}{2}$ of tortillas in chicken juices, $\frac{1}{2}$ the chicken, $\frac{1}{2}$ soup mix. Repeat and top with cheese. Chill 24 hours or freeze. Bake 1 hour at 300°.

FIX AHEAD FOOD (Continued)

MAIN DISHES (Continued)

Swiss Steak
2 lbs round steak (pound thin and cut into serving pieces)
½ C flour   1 C Catsup
Garlic Salt   1 C Water or Wine
2 onions slices   1 Bay Leaf

Heat oil in skillet. Dredge meat pieces in flour and brown on both sides. Add garlic salt, onions, catsup, water and bay leaf and simmer 45 min. Stir often, add water if necessary. Cool and freeze. Serve with mashed potatoes when reheated.

Meatloaf
2 slices soft bread   1 onion—chopped
¼ C milk   fine
2 lbs hamburger   1 tsp. garlic salt
1 egg   2 Tbls. Dijon mustard
1 pkg Knorr Green Peppercorn Sauce

Soak bread with beaten egg and milk. Add remaining ingredients and mix thoroughly. Shape into loaf and wrap in plastic to freeze. Bake in baking disk 45 min. at 350°. Prepare sauce and pour on top.

Baked Chicken and Stuffing
6 Chicken Breasts or leg/thighs
1 pkg Stove-top Stuffing Mix
1 pkg Knorr Hunter Sauce

Arrange chicken on a cookie sheet covered with foil skin-side-up. Bake 40 min. at 350° or until done. Meanwhile, prepare stuffing mix and Hunter sauce. Spread stuffing in a greased baking dish. Place baked chicken on top and pour sauce over chicken. Freeze to reheat.

Scallops
2 lbs Bay Scallops
1 stick butter or margarine
3 cloves garlic—crushed
1 can Cream of Mushroom soup
3 green onions, chopped

Saute garlic in butter 1 minute. Add Scallops and saute for 5 minutes or until tender. Add soup, heat and top with onions. Freeze or serve with rice.

OTHER MAIN DISHES (to freeze)

Spaghetti   Chili   *Stew (without potatoes)
*Cooked potatoes do not freeze well unless they are mashed or blended with other ingredients.

Save Some Fat Tips

INSTEAD OF:	USE:	AND SAVE (IN FAT CALORIES):
regular salad dressing	fat-free salad dressing	50 per Tbs
mayonnaise	fat-free mayonnaise	100 per Tbs
margarine	fat-free margarine	100 per Tbs
sour cream	fat-free sour cream	30 per Tbs
cream cheese	fat-free cream cheese	100 per oz
Provolone cheese	part-skim Mozzarella	30 per oz
eggs	egg substitute	48 per egg
oil (in baking)	applesauce (same amt.)	360 per 1/4 cup oil
oil	pan spray	120 per Tbs

Reference: Bellerson, Karen J. The Complete & Up-to-Date Fat Book. New York: Avery Publishing Group.
Prepared by Diane M. De Baise, MS, RD

FIX AHEAD FOOD (Continued)

VEGETABLES

Bake vegetable casseroles then cool; cut into squares, and freeze in foil or plastic. Open foil on a cookie sheet or put plastic in microwave and heat—no cleanup!

Broccoli Squares
Cook broccoli until almost done. Place in greased casserole dish.

Blend, 1 can cream of chicken soup with $\frac{1}{2}$ can milk, pour over broccoli.

Melt 6 tbls butter with $\frac{2}{3}$ cup hot water and pour over 1 pkg. croutons. Spread on top of broccoli and press down. Bake at 350° for 45 min.

Corn Pudding Squares
Combine a 20 oz. bag frozen corn with 3 eggs and 1 diced onion. Mix $\frac{1}{4}$ cup flour, 2 tsp. salt, $\frac{1}{4}$ tsp. pepper, 1 tbls. sugar, and a dash of nutmeg. Stir into corn mixture. Add 2 tbls. melted butter, 2 cups cream and 1 can chopped pimientos. Pour into a shallow $1\frac{1}{2}$ qt. greased baking dish. Set dish in pan and pour hot water to 1 inch depth. Bake uncovered 1 hour at 350°. Cool and cut into squares to freeze.

NOODLES

Noodles freeze well in individual portions or in family sized dishes for entrees, after school snacks, or side dishes.

Fettucine Alfredo
1–8 oz. pkg. noodles
$\frac{1}{2}$ cup melted butter
$\frac{1}{2}$ cup grated parmesan cheese
$\frac{1}{2}$ cup light cream

Cook noodles in boiling water with $\frac{1}{2}$ tsp oil. Drain. Place noodles in skillet with melted butter, add parmesan cheese and cream. Stir and top with more cheese. Refrigerate in skillet. Cut and freeze.

POTATOES

It requires the same amount of gas or electricity to bake one potato as it takes to bake ten!

Stuffed Potatoes
Scoop out well baked potatoes.
Blend in:
  Sour cream/dressing
  Chopped onion
  Grated cheddar cheese
  Drained tuna
  Salt and pepper

Stuff mixture into potato shells, top with more cheese, wrap in foil—freeze. Reheat in a hot oven or in microwave.

QUICKIE SIDE DISHES (to serve with casseroles)

1. Salad: 1 can green beans, chopped tomatoes and onions in salad dressing.
2. Salad: 1 can niblets corn, cooked peas, diced celery and onion in salad dressing.
3. Salad: Pineapple, or pear, and cottage cheese
4. Vegetables: Cooked peas or green beans
5. Warm bread, or garlic toast

☐ END MAKING LUNCHES DAILY!

A large loaf of bread has 20 slices which equals 10 sandwiches.

Take one hour each weekend to fix and freeze sandwiches for the week. Remove sandwiches from the freezer each morning and they will be defrosted by lunchtime.

BREAD: Buy each family member a loaf of their favorite bread, and teach them to make their own sandwiches. Offer a variety such as pita bread, onion or french rolls and hamburger or hot dog buns.

FILLINGS: Peanut butter, ham, bologna, salami, turkey, chicken, pastrami, roast beef or pork, and tuna made with sour cream or dressing freeze well.

CONDIMENTS: Use only condiments that will freeze. Don't use mayonnaise. You can add variety to sandwiches by using butter, jam or jelly, mustard, relish, catsup, BBQ sauce, honey, chutney, horseradish sauce, sour cream, salad dressing, teriyaki sauce, sweet and sour sauce or cranberry sauce. They all freeze well.

WRAPPING: Freeze sandwiches in separate plastic bags. Make sure you label the sandwich, and who it was made for. Date sandwiches if you think they won't be eaten right away. Placing sandwiches in a large airtight bag will preserve them longer.

ADD A TOUCH OF FRESHNESS

Prepare individual bags of lettuce, sprouts, cheese, onion, tomato or pickles that can be added just before eating.

☐ MEAL TIPS TO SAVE TIME

(end the fast food syndrome)

If you are the cook, your life can be easier by making a few simple changes when you prepare meals and give yourself permission to have "take-out" food when your budget permits. A positive attitude toward change will help you save on meal preparation time. Complete this exercise to determine if you can save time. If you circle a 5, you are saying you will try this tip. If you circle a 1, you are saying this tip won't work for you.

	AGREE				DISAGREE
Planning meals a week ahead will provide more nutritious meals	5	4	3	2	1
The food section of the newspaper will be saved until I'm ready to plan the shopping	5	4	3	2	1
Coupons should be cut and organized by category, to save time and money	5	4	3	2	1
A weekly menu posted on the refrigerator will eliminate morning decisions regarding dinner plans	5	4	3	2	1
Shopping with a grocery list will save time and money	5	4	3	2	1
Time and money can be saved by buying in bulk and having individual portions wrapped (chicken, chops, etc.)	5	4	3	2	1
Raw chicken parts, chops and hamburgers can be flash frozen on a cookie sheet and stored in plastic bags	5	4	3	2	1
By buying bulk hamburger and freezing smaller individual portions I'll be prepared to fix tacos, spaghetti, etc.	5	4	3	2	1
I can fry hamburger to freeze for future casseroles while unpacking groceries	5	4	3	2	1
Preparing double recipes saves a future meal preparation when I freeze one with a label with instructions for the oven or microwave	5	4	3	2	1

	AGREE			DISAGREE	
I can bake or BBQ extra chicken to keep in the freezer for salads, sandwiches or entrees	5	4	3	2	1
It's easy to boil some extra noodles or spaghetti and freeze them for future dishes	5	4	3	2	1
I will build a fresh supply of sandwiches by preparing them immediately after dinner with leftover meat	5	4	3	2	1
Building future dinners from leftovers will keep a reserve of meals in the freezer	5	4	3	2	1
Identical storage devices such as plastic containers, foil pans, and glass dishes will stack to save freezer space	5	4	3	2	1
I can make extra cookie dough to freeze for the children to slice and bake	5	4	3	2	1
Cooking an occasional turkey can provide surplus meat for sandwiches, soup, main dishes and salads	5	4	3	2	1
I will devote at least one hour each week to advance meal preparation	5	4	3	2	1
After practicing these tips for a few weeks I should be able to skip a week of major grocery shopping once each month	5	4	3	2	1

TOTAL

If you scored above 60, you are ready to save time and money. If you rated yourself between 40 and 60, you have some reservations about devoting time to meal preparation. A rating of less than 25 indicates you are not ready to address your meal planning habits or have other ways to keep this area balanced.

CREATE A STANDARD "QUICKIE" MEAL TO PREPARE FOR "UNEXPECTED GUEST" DINNERS

Example: Step 1 40 minutes RICE: Prepare a package mix as directed

Step 2 30 minutes CHICKEN: Saute parts in butter until done

Step 3 10 minutes GREEN BEANS: French style. Prepare frozen package as directed.

Step 4 10 minutes SALAD: Tossed greens

Step 5 5 minutes CHEESE SAUCE: Dry package mix. Prepare as directed.

Assemble green beans on a platter, arrange chicken parts on beans, pour cheese sauce over all and top with bacon bits.

Serve with salad, rice, rolls and wine.

This meal takes 45 minutes—from grocery bag to the table.

FIX A "QUICKIE MEAL" WHEN YOU HAVE TO EAT AND RUN

(Keep these ingredients on hand for the emergency)

MEXICAN MINUTE MEAL	MAC-TUNA

Combine in 2 qt. pot:
  1 Can *Chile and Beans*
  1 Can *Enchilada Sauce*
  1 Can *Tomato Sauce*
  4 C crushed *Tortilla Chips*
 	
Heat thoroughly, then add:
  2 C grated *Cheddar Cheese*
until melted
 	
Serve with sliced tomatoes and cucumbers.
	Prepare in a 2 qt. pot:
	  1 pkg Macaroni and Cheese
	
	Add:
	  1 Can drained Tuna
	  1 pkg. frozen Peas
	
	Heat until peas are done.
	
	Serve with carrot sticks and toast.

DEVELOP YOUR OWN REFERENCE LIBRARY ON SURVIVAL SKILLS FOR THE HOME FRONT

"CONQUERING THE PAPER PILE-UP"

Stephanie Culp
Writers Digest Books, Cincinatti, Ohio
How to sort, organize files and store every piece of paper in your home and office.

"FIVE DAYS TO AN ORGANIZED LIFE"

Lucy A. Hedrick
Dell Publishing Div. of Bantam Doubleday Dell Publishing Group, Inc., New York
Get rid of the chaos in your life in five days by learning what to do and how to do it.

"FROM STRESS TO STRENGTH"

Robert S. Eliot, M.D.
Bantam Doubleday Dell Publishing Group, Inc., New York
How to lighten your load and save your heart and your life.

"GET THE FAT OUT"

Victoria Moran
Crown Publishing, Inc., New York
501 tips to get the fat out of your life.

"JENNIFER LANG COOKS FOR KIDS"

Jennifer Lang
Crown Publishing, Inc., New York
153 recipes and ideas for good food that kids love to eat.

DEVELOP YOUR OWN REFERENCE LIBRARY
(Continued)

"PARENTS BOOK OF CHILD SAFETY"

David Laskin
Ballatine Books, New York
From preparing the nursery through school life, you can keep your
child safe at home, outdoors, in the car, in school and on vacation.

"PRACTICAL PARENTING TIPS"

Vicki Lansky
Meadowbook Press, New York
Ideas for childproofing, tantrums, feeding, sleeping, clothing, sibling
rivalry, and getting gum out of hair.

"THE WORKING FAMILY'S COOKBOOK"

Irena Chalmers
Barron's Educational Series, Inc., Hauppauge, New York
Beautifully illustrated, 250 easy recipes that can be prepared in 20–60
minutes with shopping lists, in a 3-ring binder.

"THE 10 MINUTE SHOPPER"

Martin Sloane
Berkley Publishing Group, New York
Tips, tricks and techniques for people who hate to grocery shop.
Whether you're single, married or have a family, this book will save
time and anxiety at the supermarket.

"365 EASY ONE-DISH MEALS"

Natalie Haughton
Harper & Row, Publishers, New York
Recipes for hassle-free, one pot to clean cooking, when time is short.

CHECK YOUR PROGRESS IN HOMEFRONT ISSUES

Now that you have examined your homefront activities and explored the benefits of getting organized, identify action you can take to improve your home balance and better manage at work.

Responsibilities I can delegate: _____

_____

Expectations I can eliminate: _____

_____

New tasks I will teach someone else: _____

_____

Expectations I need to communicate: _____

_____

Areas my attitude must be more positive: _____

_____

Things I will organize better: _____

_____

Some of my work can be done by: _____

_____

If you were able to list specific actions on one or more of the above issues, congratulations! This indicates you are serious about making positive improvements at home.

CAREER:
CHECK CAREER BALANCE

> Every ego needs to be fed. Some are hungrier than others. The pursuit of a successful CAREER can cause you to let go of other aspects of your life.
>
> You must strive to maintain values and relationships to insure your daily activities do not get out of balance.

out of balance

CASE #2: THE MISSING RELATIONSHIP

(SINGLE PERSON)

When John was promoted to the position of supervisor of his department, he met the challenge with enthusiasm. With hard work and some creative ideas, he led his unit to the top of production. He has always maintained a high level of performance during business hours but discovered that by taking work home he could accomplish even more. After several months, John is beginning to feel burned out and needs a new challenge.

After his promotion, John discontinued the regular evening workouts he had been doing at the gym. His physical condition has suffered. Since the promotion, he has gained weight and it's common for him to fall asleep in front of the television. He also cannot seem to finish the novel he started last summer.

John's career has also impacted his relationship with his girlfriend, Joanne. They used to enjoy outdoor activities together on weekends which gave him an opportunity to hike, ski and fish, some of his favorite forms of relaxation. Things cooled off when he started putting increased energy into his career. She called him a few times, but no longer calls.

John took a hard look at himself last Sunday and decided his lifestyle had become too boring and predictable. He wants to change it. He wants to lose some weight and start having more fun. He isn't sure where to start.

What steps would you recommend that John take towards a better balance in his home and career?

Compare your answers with the author's suggestions on page 83.

PEOPLE MEASURE SUCCESS IN DIFFERENT WAYS AND ENJOY THE BENEFITS BECAUSE. . .

— Some devote time to building human relationships

— Others seize opportunities to fulfill their potential

— There are those who are careful not to rob the homefront when pursuing a career

— Many are positive about their work and take pride in setting high goals

— A few are committed to success in their chosen field

— Some individuals are able to do all of the above.

— Lots of people have found that the services of professionals are helping them achieve success when they are feeling stress between home and career. See page 79 for details.

TWO WAYS TO MEASURE

A JOB   =   PAYCHECK

A CAREER   =   FULFILLMENT

#1 MEASURE YOUR PERFORMANCE AT WORK

You can be successful at your job and prove to yourself and others it is still possible to balance your life. YOU control your performance! Being an interested employee creates a positive environment which is easier to balance than a negative one. Select three things from the following list to work on in order to become a better employee.

I will:

_____ Think about the value of a positive attitude in my work.

_____ Acknowledge the consequences of being late or absent. (This includes returning late from lunches and breaks.) Managers should consider their role modeling.

_____ Establish priorities for different tasks I perform.

_____ Improve communications with my boss and peers.

_____ Avoid the rumor mill.

_____ Work to improve my listening skills.

_____ Admit mistakes and learn from them.

_____ Practice professionalism by grooming and dressing for the role I want, not the role I have.

_____ Learn to be flexible and accept change.

_____ Schedule monthly or quarterly meetings with my supervisor to communicate progress and evaluate annual goals.

_____ _____

(add your own)

Your desire to succeed in your current position is communicated through your attitude, performance, flexibility and the amount of energy you demonstrate on the job. Being able to identify areas in which you can improve is a good first step to becoming a better employee.

> SUCCESS NEVER COMES
> TO THOSE WHO SIMPLY WAIT
> FOR IT!

#2 MEASURE YOUR PERFORMANCE AGAINST WHAT YOUR BOSS EXPECTS

All employers have expectations. Some have them in writing, others communicate what they expect verbally. Too often expectations fail to be communicated at all, in which case the responsibility to find out what is expected falls on the employee.

Following are some tips that will help you see your job from your employer's point of view.

PERSONNEL ADMINISTRATION—Every employer from a small business to large corporation has policies that employees and the company are expected to follow. Some companies are mandated by the government to know where there is management discretion in the application of policies. You should know what channel to follow and seek guidance through your Human Resources department. Clear communication with your boss about such issues as work hours, length of breaks, absenteeism, vacations, personal time, overtime, etc. is absolutely necessary in order for you to live up to the expectations.

KNOWLEDGE/SKILL—Employers expect that the degree of knowledge and skill you were hired with will be applied on the job and competence will increase over time by additional training so that you become a more valuable employee. You cannot wait for your supervisor to identify training opportunities. You should take responsibility for your own development and seek guidance from your supervisor.

PRODUCTION—Expectations in production must be clearly communicated. They may need to be developed over time, however, it is best to have expectations and goals documented in writing to use as a reference when you have monthly or quarterly update meetings with your supervisor. You can take responsibility for the documentation if your supervisor doesn't. Whether you work independently, or as part of a team, meeting or exceeding the production goals will be reflected in your performance evaluation. Remember that what you produce is also part of your boss' overall evaluation.

GROWTH AND EXPERIENCE—Most employers expect you to seek new learning in your career. Discuss cross training and future opportunities with your boss. If promotions happen infrequently in your company, look for lateral moves and opportunities to offer your time and assistance which will give you growth and experience.

HOW DOES YOUR COMPANY MEASURE UP?

The following points could help you build rapport with your supervisor and feel good about your company.

* As COMMUNICATIONS are being established with your supervisor you should share home responsibilities that impact your ability to produce when they are neglected. Be honest about why you request time off.

* CHANGE creates anxiety and resistance, however when it occurs being positive and receptive will result in a more effective outcome and reduce your stress.

* To increase your KNOWLEDGE AND SKILL you can take the initiative and demonstrate a willingness to learn and accept new challenges.

* PRODUCTION is important. To achieve the maximum production each day, you may want to learn about time management skills to help you produce the most important work first.

* ILLNESS ALLOWANCE is for when you are sick, not a means to gain additional time off. Recognize that when you are routinely absent or late it may be interpreted as poor performance or that you are not a supportive team member.

IMPROVE YOUR PRODUCTIVITY

Most people are hired to produce a product or a service. Performance is usually measured by the quality and quantity you produce. When you accept the challenge to increase your productivity you may find that whatever you contribute often is returned twofold. Hooray for rewards!

TIP #1: LET OTHERS HELP YOU

Some things you can do for yourself. The responsibility is yours. Check those items you have under control:

____ Arrive early and be ready to start on time

____ Maintain a positive attitude

____ Read everything possible about my job, company and industry

____ Ask questions relevant to my job

____ Increase my pace and do more than my share

____ Attend classes that enhance knowledge and performance

____ Put in a full day by minimizing "breaks"—and not leaving early

Your peers play an important role in your development. It is your job to build positive working relationships with them. Check growth items that are available through your peers:

____ Listen to their experience in the business

____ Participate in training—from them and for them

____ Encourage teamwork for more productivity

____ Lend support for peers when job demands it

____ Demonstrate why quality production is important to all

____ Create an environment conducive to productivity

Usually your supervisor will expect your productivity to steadily increase over time. When those expectations are not being communicated, you must find out what he or she can do to enhance your performance. Check areas you can ask your supervisor to help increase your productivity:

____ Ask what cross-training opportunities are available

____ Request feedback on your performance

____ Learn pitfalls to be avoided

____ Solicit your supervisors' knowledge and experience

____ Look for example of good role models

____ Learn what rewards are available for superior effort

TIP #2: COMMUTING

Commuting offers downtime for thinking, relaxing or preparing your day or evening. Regardless of how you commute to work, you can put that time to productive use if you choose. If you commute by car, DRIVE SAFELY. If you use public transportation, consider the comfort of your fellow commuters during the trip. Here are some things you can do to use the time wisely. Check those which relate to you. Add your own ideas.

General

_____ Organize your day

_____ Prepare a "to do" list

_____ Plan meals

_____ Create a shopping list

_____ Jot down unfinished business

_____ Plan a party

_____ Create a phone list

_____ _____
(add your own)

When commuting by car:

_____ Tape record letters and memos

_____ Listen to educational tapes

_____ Sing with the radio

_____ _____
(add your own)

_____ Use car phone to eliminate some necessary calls at home or work

Using public transportation:

_____ Do paperwork

_____ Read the newspaper

_____ Write/plan

_____ _____
(add your own)

(Any other ideas):

_____   _____

TIP #3: USE YOUR LUNCHTIME PRODUCTIVELY

Many things can be accomplished during your lunchbreak to help you balance your career and home life. Plan something different every day at lunch to add variety. Lunch is an ideal time to take care of brief personal errands that would otherwise be a distraction.

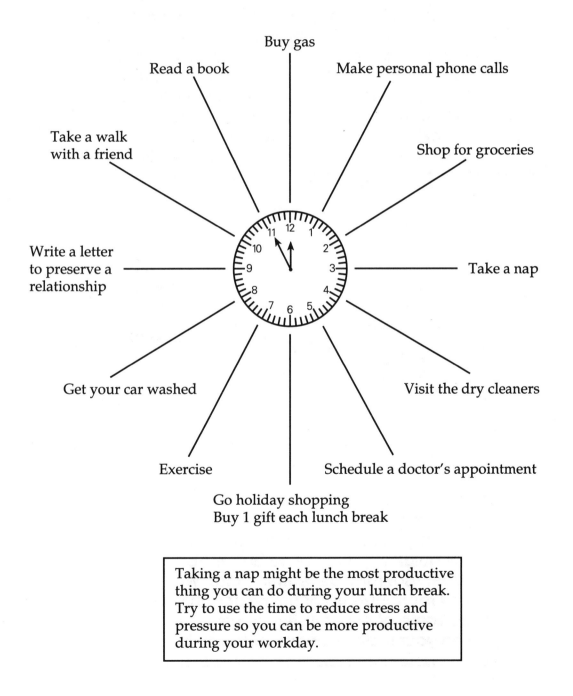

Buy gas

Read a book

Make personal phone calls

Take a walk with a friend

Shop for groceries

Write a letter to preserve a relationship

Take a nap

Get your car washed

Visit the dry cleaners

Exercise

Schedule a doctor's appointment

Go holiday shopping
Buy 1 gift each lunch break

Taking a nap might be the most productive thing you can do during your lunch break. Try to use the time to reduce stress and pressure so you can be more productive during your workday.

HOW UNDERSTANDING SHOULD YOUR SUPERVISOR BE?
(If you're a supervisor, this will be of interest to you)

As a parent you may need special consideration when your children have extra needs. Communicating with your supervisor is essential so you clearly understand any limitations, company policies, and what is expected of you. This may have been covered during your interview, orientation, or training. If not, you need to take responsibility to know what behavior is acceptable in your organization so that your performance will meet the standards of your company and your boss.

A QUIZ WITH ANSWERS

Unless you please your supervisor, things will quickly get out of balance. Your supervisor may be learning too. When you recognize his or her responsibilities and do some of the adjusting yourself, you will find your supervisor can help you balance.

YOUR SUPERVISOR HAS EXPECTATIONS

Some supervisors have experienced parenting, others have not. Those with experience may be more supportive in helping you work through difficult times. All supervisors, however, have a responsibility to their company to produce a product or service, and to their employees to partner with them in finding solutions for work coverage. Most managers have been trained to treat employees identically and not to address individual requests for flexibility. Many companies are experimenting with flex-time (adjusting work hours), work at home and job sharing programs. Managers and supervisors are learning about how to treat employees individual needs in balancing their work and family needs. The following steps can help when you are feeling that a family need is beginning to conflict with your supervisors expectations:

- Become aware of your business/corporate culture and what policies exist for paid/unpaid time off and schedule flexibility.

- Determine which behaviors your supervisor considers to be a demonstration of commitment within your business/corporate culture.

- Communicate with your supervisor about your family/child care needs and expectations. Especially if there is a severe penalty for picking up children late from day care.

- Have a back-up plan to insure proper care when your child or sitter is sick.

- If you are a new mother, be honest and realistic about when you plan to return to work based on what you know and feel at the moment. Supervisors need to adjust production with you.

- If elder care is becoming a concern for you, inquire with your Human Resources department, local hospital, non-profit agencies or Personal Assistance Program referral for guidance.

- Instruct older children who are alone after school how to let you know they have arrived safely and what to do in an emergency. Create a system for them to communicate with you about non-emergency topics that will not interfere with your production.

CHECK YOUR CAREER ATTITUDE

Now that you have explored some of the things that influence your career, check ways you can improve on the job.

I can:

_____ Be a more responsible employee and improve my productivity.

_____ Use commute time to utilize my time more efficiently.

_____ Spend my lunchtime more productively.

_____ Plan time to take care of unusual problems so that my productively will not be affected.

_____ Plan ahead for routine "emergencies" that are part of my parental responsibilities.

_____ Be understanding with others having parental responsibilities.

_____ Identify and practice behaviors that support the concept of teamwork, within your company culture.

LEISURE:
BUILD IN LEISURE ACTIVITIES

An employee with an enriching personal life is often a more effective worker. Some feel, however, that LEISURE time is unproductive. Since the goal of working is to produce a product or service, they view time spent on relaxing activities a waste of time or an exercise in laziness. Research however, shows that leisure activities help clear the air, rejuvenate a tired body and create a more motivated, satisfied person at home <u>and</u> at work.

out of balance

CASE #3: THE BUSY COUPLE

Mary is manager of the advertising department for a large bank. She has just been assigned a new project that will require a lot of time and energy. She needs to hire three additional people and train them. She has been working long hours and taking work home at night. In addition, the Gilbert and Sullivan group she belongs to wants her to accept a nomination for the presidency. It will require a commitment of ten hours a month, plus a variety of events throughout the year. Mary's routine is exhausting. At the end of the day all she wants to do is eat, relax and go to bed.

Mary's husband Mark has a non-demanding job and is never too tired to play in the evenings and on weekends. He is a serious amateur photographer and wants Mary to accompany him two to three weekends a month on photography excursions. They are a good team and always have a good time together and she is creative and helpful scouting out subject matter and assisting him. Other couples sometimes join them. These weekends prevent Mark and Mary from the weekly chores of laundry, cleaning and shopping which are still waiting to be done when they go back to work on Monday morning. With no food in the house, and busy schedules, Mary and Mark eat out frequently or bring home fried chicken. Both have gained ten pounds in the last year.

Mark has been the Activity Chairman for his photography club for the past three years. The cost of his hobby has strained their budget and now he wants to join a golf and tennis club. Mark want to entertain friends in the evening or go bowling. He can't understand Mary's lack of enthusiasm.

What steps would you recommend that Mark and Mary take to develop a better partnership and balance between their home and careers?

See author's solutions on page 84.

Time for fun doesn't just surface. You need to plan for it. Activities that are considered relaxing; a release from stress; or entertaining are different for each person. Communicate your selection of "Happiness Factors" to friends, co-workers and family. You will then build a support system and might even find others who would enjoy the activity with you.

FUN ADDS
TO THE HAPPINESS

Leisure time activity is often determined by the amount of people contact you have on the job. If your job includes considerable interpersonal contact, you may desire some quiet activity during your time off. If your job requires little contact with people, you will probably want more social activities.

A "HAPPINESS FACTOR" is an activity that helps you relax, enjoy a sense of enrichment, or simply makes you feel good. Everybody has happiness factors. From the following list, <u>check</u> the things you enjoy. Then plan time each day for at least one item.

_____	Pursue a hobby	_____	Garden
_____	Study investments	_____	Visit a lounge
_____	Read a book	_____	Join a community group
_____	Create a meal	_____	Enroll in a class
_____	Exercise	_____	Assist a youth group
_____	Watch television	_____	Attend a sports event
_____	Start a collection	_____	Create handiwork
_____	Go shopping	_____	Repair something
_____	Redecorate a room	_____	(add yours) _____
_____	Enjoy music	_____	_____

As little as an hour a day will provide an opportunity to relax and reduce stress. If you need to calendar the specific activity into your day—DO IT! If you prefer, just allocate certain hours at the beginning or end of your day to relax with your favorite activity. It's important to introduce a variety of "happiness factors" during your personal time to provide several outlets for stress.

FORECAST TIME FOR FUN AND RELAXATION

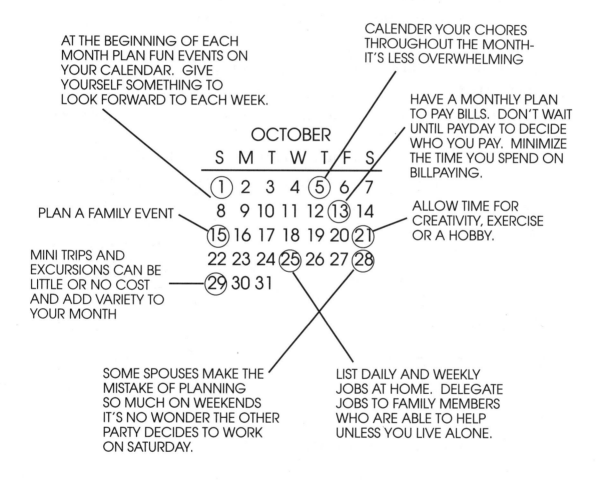

AT THE BEGINNING OF EACH MONTH PLAN FUN EVENTS ON YOUR CALENDAR. GIVE YOURSELF SOMETHING TO LOOK FORWARD TO EACH WEEK.

CALENDER YOUR CHORES THROUGHOUT THE MONTH- IT'S LESS OVERWHELMING

HAVE A MONTHLY PLAN TO PAY BILLS. DON'T WAIT UNTIL PAYDAY TO DECIDE WHO YOU PAY. MINIMIZE THE TIME YOU SPEND ON BILLPAYING.

OCTOBER

S	M	T	W	T	F	S
1	2	3	4	5	6	7
8	9	10	11	12	13	14
15	16	17	18	19	20	21
22	23	24	25	26	27	28
29	30	31				

PLAN A FAMILY EVENT

ALLOW TIME FOR CREATIVITY, EXERCISE OR A HOBBY.

MINI TRIPS AND EXCURSIONS CAN BE LITTLE OR NO COST AND ADD VARIETY TO YOUR MONTH

SOME SPOUSES MAKE THE MISTAKE OF PLANNING SO MUCH ON WEEKENDS IT'S NO WONDER THE OTHER PARTY DECIDES TO WORK ON SATURDAY.

LIST DAILY AND WEEKLY JOBS AT HOME. DELEGATE JOBS TO FAMILY MEMBERS WHO ARE ABLE TO HELP UNLESS YOU LIVE ALONE.

TAKE TIME FOR FUN AND SELF GRATIFICATION

Commit personal time to a purpose that allows some form of relaxation. To help you experience a variety of activities during personal time, check the items that you will include in next month's calendar.

RECREATION

☐ Pursue a new hobby or activate a former one
☐ Establish or maintain a regular exercise program
☐ Learn a new sport
☐ Allocate time to be creative through handiwork

FAMILY TIME

☐ Plan ahead for TV watching. Other nights plan activities that allow for family interaction
☐ Identify one day each month for home clean-up and yardwork
☐ Attend a sports or entertainment event together at least twice a month
☐ Allocate time to do things with children

TIME ALONE

☐ Read a book or watch television
☐ Be creative through cooking
☐ Study a topic to develop new knowledge
☐ Repair something

COMMUNICATING

☐ Go shopping with a friend
☐ Join a community group
☐ Enroll in a class
☐ Call someone you haven't talked with in a long time

BUILDING RELATIONSHIPS

☐ Assist with a volunteer group
☐ Invite a new friend or co-worker to dinner
☐ Visit with a neighbor
☐ Spend time alone with your "significant other"

Note: It's okay to do *absolutely nothing*. In today's society we often feel pressure to fill every minute with productive activity. Allow time for nothing.

ONLY THOSE WILLING TO CONSIDER THEIR PHYSICAL NEEDS WILL ACHIEVE SATISFACTION

Physical exercise is essential for good mental health because it provides an outlet for stress. You can balance your home and career easier when you get regular physical exercise.

When planning your monthly calendar, allocate time for exercise. You will discover that following a good workout you have patience and can cope better.

FOUR STEPS TO PHYSICAL FITNESS

| STEP 1 | — IDENTIFY your options

Explore opportunities for regular exercise. This may mean joining a class or club, purchasing equipment, or collecting information about where to locate other enthusiasts.

| STEP 2 | — SELECT the possibilities

Decide what types of physical exercise you would most enjoy, (consider health guidelines, your resources, your allocation of time, and cost).

| STEP 3 | — COMMIT yourself to one or more activities.

Sign up, buy what you need and tell your friends and family what you plan to do and when. The activity will become more of an accountability and you'll get involved.

| STEP 4 | — FOLLOW THROUGH

Calendar the time you have committed to physical exercise. Consider doing your activity with a friend to help insure commitment. Make it a priority to always show up if you join a group.

> Experts agree that by following these easy steps you will be able to stay healthy, feel less stress and cope better on a daily basis.

HOW TO REACH A SUCCESSFUL BALANCE

You can maximize your ability to balance all three elements of life when you learn the formula shown on the next page. Don't expect to create the perfect balance overnight. You will probably need to make a few changes at a time and adjust to them before making others.

A FORMULA
FOR BALANCE

The three elements of your life are heavily influenced by attitude and the way you communicate.

$$\frac{\text{HOME} + \text{CAREER} + \text{LEISURE}}{\text{ATTITUDE} + \text{COMMUNICATION}} = \text{BALANCE}$$

Happy people still feel frustration and become irritated at times. Their basic satisfaction with life however, remains intact. You know your life has better balance when you function well not only when things are going right, but also you can keep going when things go wrong.

SURVIVING THE CHALLENGE OF:

- life in the fast lane

- parenthood merry-go-round

- single parent stress

- being involved in too many activities

- poor balance between home, career and/or personal life

> It's easier to cope when you apply some creativity to those areas that cause stress and anxiety.

CREATIVE WAYS TO IMPROVE YOUR BALANCE

Check those ideas that will help improve your balance.

_____ "Detach" yourself slightly from your work environment in order to become more objective.

_____ Compliment your supervisor for her/his contribution when he/she helps you balance.

_____ Buy birthday, anniversary, and special event cards in advance. Pre-address and sign them. Mark them in a calendar so you will remember to send them.

_____ Buy gift items ahead for the same reason; make the most of sales and one-stop shopping.

_____ Employ a retired person to do your grocery shopping. They will be able to take advantage of best hours, coupons. Smart shopping by them will help pay for their cost.

_____ Next time you get a raise, establish a direct deposit to a special savings account to be used only for "leisure balancing" purposes.

_____ Assign different responsibility for an evening meal preparation each weekend.

_____ Declare the first 10 minutes after your arrival from work as a "time out."

_____ Take your number one "human problem" out for breakfast once each month for counseling and theraputic conversation.

_____ _____

(add your own)

If you have children, following are some ideas to have them help you cope. Check those you will try:

_____ Designate a laundry day for each family member to "own" the washer and dryer for his or her laundry.

_____ Assign one night a week for each teenager or older family member to plan and prepare the evening meal.

_____ Take each child to breakfast or lunch once a month to allow for solid one to one communication.

_____ Establish a family event that teenagers control. Go camping or rent a cabin from which you can commute to work. Let them handle all of the plans and do the cooking.

_____ _____

(create your own)

SPECIAL SECTION

(IF YOU DON'T HAVE CHILDREN,
YOU MAY WANT TO SKIP TO PAGE 71)

Many people need to get their act together when it comes to children. Below are some tips to save time and help get you to HOME PLATE.

CHILD CARE: Select child care that is consistent with your views on eating, sleeping, toilet training and TV time. Provide work phone numbers, doctor's number, medical release form and written instructions. Tell your doctor who cares for your children. Leave a supply of food and diapers with your sitter and replenish as needed. Communicate privately to get an accounting of your child's daily activities. Always keep your sitter advised about what has happened at home. Have a plan when illness occurs to insure the child receives proper care.

HOUSEHOLD NECESSITIES: Make a weekly plan for laundry, shopping and cleaning. Post a weekly menu plan and shopping list. Select clothing before you go to bed at night. Consider hiring help with housekeeping to relieve stress and anxiety. If your sitter comes to your home, you may be able to pay a little extra to do laundry and cleaning. When family members help, don't insist that they do it your way. Be grateful and flexible.

PERSONAL WELFARE: Collect everything you need to take with you the next day and put it in the car or by the door before going to bed. Children can help. Personal phone calls to and from your care-giver should be based on necessity. Both have a responsibility to their job. Plan 15 minutes a day for yourself.

PARENT/CHILD RELATIONSHIPS: Maintain good communication by spending time alone with each child everyday. Do the same at least one evening a week with your spouse. After childbirth, returning to work will be easier if you can work part-time for the first few weeks. Parents could alternate taking children to the doctor. Plan entertainment for children during your commute. Regularly do something your child wants to do.

> Raising children creates another dimension in your balancing act. Remember that these years are temporary and provide for tremendous personal growth during this special time.

BUILDING SELF-ESTEEM IN YOUR CHILD

Here are ten ways your child can begin to develop a sense of character and independence. Measure how well you are teaching your child to take responsibility by completing the following exercise:

		ALWAYS	SOMETIMES	NEVER
1.	I praise my child for trying to help	___	___	___
2.	When my child does chores, I don't expect performance at adult standards	___	___	___
3.	I communicate with my child about being responsible (homework, being on time, fulfilling commitments) to create a responsible attitude	___	___	___
4.	I encourage my child to assist with meals by providing opportunities he or she can handle	___	___	___
5.	I plan simple meals with easy directions to follow	___	___	___
6.	Guideline for making beds and picking up clothes and toys are clear and understood	___	___	___
7.	I allow my child to make several decisions about what to wear, what to eat and how to spend free time	___	___	___
8.	I assist my child in setting realistic goals by focusing discussions on the future	___	___	___
9.	When my child experiences achievement, he or she receives praise	___	___	___
10.	I provide a reward at the end of the week when goals are met.	___	___	___
	TOTALS	___	___	___

If you scored highest in the category marked:

ALWAYS = Good for you! Your child should develop a healthy character
SOMETIMES = Try giving your child more space to become responsible
NEVER = Practice letting go until it feels comfortable and help your child grow into a responsible person

EXPLORE YOUR OPTIONS
IN CHILD CARE ARRANGEMENTS

Wise parents consider options for possible things that can occur. Your plan should allow you to pursue your career and/or personal time without guilt. You need to be comfortable with your selection of child care in order to feel a sense of balance. Sitters, teachers and grandparents have experience with children, so hire an expert to help you when necessary. Identify your child care options from the following list:

	Yes	Maybe	No
Spouse	___	___	___
Grandparent	___	___	___
Sitter at home	___	___	___
Sitter in their home	___	___	___
Religious day care center—non-profit	___	___	___
Franchised operations—profit making	___	___	___
Parent co-op	___	___	___
Nursery school	___	___	___
Government funded day care	___	___	___
Day camp—summer and school holidays	___	___	___
Other	___	___	___

Research all possibilities. Many options provide excellent care, but are ignored because parents don't know they exist. Explore until you find a source that agrees with your views on child rearing and meets your standards of cleanliness and responsibility.

REFERENCE: "The Day Care Kit" a parents guide to finding quality child care. Deborah Spaide, General Publishing Co. Limited, Don Mills, Ontario. An excellent guide to selecting, maintaining quality day care for your child as well as referral sources, tax implications and an abuse resource guide.

STEPS TO CHOOSING DAY CARE

List all day care providers or centers you intend to pre-screen and interview. In addition, conduct "pop-visits" by stopping in when they are not expecting you. This will give you an opportunity to assess things under regular conditions when you are not expected.

☐ 1. Interview staff for qualifications and sensitivity to infant/children's needs and feelings.

☐ 2. Assess the environment for health and safety such as crib/beds, bathrooms and play areas.

☐ 3. Inspect toys and equipment for cleanliness and repair.

☐ 4. Evaluate equipment to develop infant education such as crib mobiles, rattles, mirrors, squeeze toys, stacking/sorting and pull toys.

☐ 5. Assess toys that develop communication skills such as books, pictures, toy phones, musical toys, dolls and puppets.

☐ 6. Analyze the equipment available for children to release emotion and anxiety such as musical mobiles, rocking chair, punching toys, soft bat and balls, dolls and clothes, and costumes.

☐ 7. Evaluate opportunities that develop large motor skills such as riding/rocking toys, climbing/sliding equipment, balls, grabbing and tossing toys.

☐ 8. Assess opportunities that develop small motor skills such as blocks, puzzles, paint, clay/Playdoh, magnetic boards, sand, cars, lacing/stacking toys.

☐ 9. Determine the daily routine. Does it include snacks/meals, rest/quiet time, music, outdoor play, large and small motor skill development, social time and time alone.

☐ 10. Ask if care-giver has and requires necessary forms to complete such as registration form, immunization form, daycare agreement, emergency medical release, medical administration form, activity/behavior report, infant feeding/sleeping/diapering record, illness warning notice.

☐ 11. Review care-givers plan to communicate infant/children's progress such as telephone calls (can you be interrupted at work, how often, and for how long?), written reports, parent conferences, in-person when you pick-up or deliver children (can care-giver afford the time then or is an evening phone call better?).

DAY CARE INTERVIEW COMPARISON

You may find it helpful to use this comparison chart as you research and analyze various care-giver's and centers.

CARE-GIVER/CENTER					
Hours available					
Location benefits					
Child/staff ratio					
Conditions/non-smoking					
Rules/require-ments					
Daily routine					
Communi-cation/pro-gress reports					
Toys/equipment					
Opportunity to visit References					
Cost					

CHECKLIST FOR WORKING PARENTS

This checklist may be helpful when preparing for the next morning departure to day-care or for an evening out.

DAILY OFFSITE DAY-CARE:

- ☐ MEDICATION

- ☐ CLOTHING (diapers, change of underwear, jacket)

- ☐ FOOD/BOTTLES (note any special needs for the day)

- ☐ TOYS (for your child and one to share)

- ☐ BEHAVIOR NOTES (let care-giver know what has happened at home)

EVENING SITTER: **TELEPHONE**

FOR PARENTS   _____

EMERGENCY #S   _____

SITTER EXPECTATIONS   _____

PARENTS EXPECTED RETURN TIME   _____

MEDICATION   _____

ACTIVITIES
MEAL/SNACK   _____

BATH   _____

TELEVISION (Show sitter how to use/restrictions/rules)

BEDTIME
TIME   _____

STORY   _____

HOUSEHOLD DUTIES
PICK-UP TOYS/GAMES   _____

DISHES   _____

BALANCING HOME, CAREER <u>AND</u> CHILDREN: THE ULTIMATE CHALLENGE

> Those who are busy pursuing a career, maintaining a home <u>and</u> raising a family face a complex balancing act. Parents act as coaches, teachers, chauffers, nurses, dieticians, listeners, organizers, decision makers, to name just a few roles during parenting years. Most, lack adequate experience to prepare them. This means parents should learn to work together to establish standards for their children and then communicate and reinforce these standards so that an appropriate balance can be achieved.

Don't be afraid to enlist the help of an outside consultant that can give you guidance. You can locate them through an Employee Assistance Program, local hospital, community college or non-profit organization. To access an Employee Assistance Program you must work for a company that offers this type of program to their employees.

CASE FOUR: THE PARENT TRAP

Maria and Joe live in a suburban area with their three children. Joe is a real estate agent and was recently honored as the leading salesperson in his office. To meet his clients needs Joe must often extend his business hours into the evening. His weekends are always busy showing homes. Because he believes in physical fitness, he runs early each morning. Joe shares household responsibilities with Maria by doing laundry, assisting the children with homework, and driving the carpool twice each week.

Maria is a computer operator for a company which has numerous deadlines. She is often required to work overtime. When neither parent can get home early enough to prepare dinner and spend time with the children before bed, they feel stressed and guilty. When it's impossible for either Joe or Maria to relieve the sitter at a normal time, Maria's mother is willing to pick up the children, take them home and prepare dinner. Maria resents not being able to stay home like her mother did, and maintain the standards of family life that she enjoyed as a child.

Maria and Joe have very little time alone together, and the family rarely has outings. Often Joe & Maria do not communicate the same standards and expectations to the children. Joe is quick to discipline them, while Maria is more lenient with what they do. The children have begun to demonstrate anxiety and stress.

What steps do you recommend Maria and Joe take to balance their home life?

Compare your ideas with the authors on page 84.

ATTENTION WOMEN:

Women have felt dis-empowered in the workplace for centuries. Coming
out of their role as a support person to the male bread winner of the family,
women now represent 70% of the American workforce. Once the heart and
soul of the home they often don't want to give up the power they have in this
domain. Many have high expectations of perfectionism in the home and are
unwilling to compromise when someone else takes on a homefront responsibility.
Women are more likely to reduce their own stress, anger and anxiety when
they learn how to let go of high standards and learn that part of the business
of surviving is to accept and tolerate the way spouses, children and hired help
do things.

RE-EVALUATE

PLAN TO EVALUATE ROLES AND RESPONSIBILITIES

Taking responsibility for a household chore or family obligation means that you "own the process" and manage it. It <u>DOESN'T</u> mean that you are "helping" the process owner. Other family members should accept the way you manage the responsibilities you own but agreement should be reached as to the standard or level of acceptance it supports.

To complete this action plan first identify your household/family responsibilities (A). Then check the appropriate box for the person who currently assumes that role (B). Next, identify where you will gather new information (C) and then redefine role distribution (D).

A. Household/family responsibilities	B. Current role				D. New role			
	My Role	Partner's Role	Children's Role	Hired Help Role	My Role	Partner's Role	Children's Role	Hired Help Role
1.								
2.								
3.								
4.								
5.								
6.								
7.								
8.								
9.								
10.								

C. Gather information from people who have researched or experienced your situation.

	YES	NO
Read books and articles		
Identify a mentor		
Network with others		
Join a support group		

SPECIAL SECTION

BALANCING FOR THOSE WHO TRAVEL OR RELOCATE

> **Those who travel experience additional challenges which can throw life out of balance.**

* **TRAVEL**
* **EXTENDED HOURS**
* **RELOCATION**

TIPS FOR TRAVELERS

BALANCING ACT FOR TRAVELERS

AIRLINES

Save money   * Plan ahead to take advantage of special fares. Incorporate a weekend for fun with a business trip. Staying over on a Saturday night can reduce airfare dramatically.

Earn awards   * Join a frequent flyer program and insure credit at check-in.

Save money   * ALWAYS charge airline tickets to a credit card. If lost or stolen, tickets can be reissued quickly with no hassle.

Maintain diet   * Ask about special meal availability. Most major airlines provide vegetarian, low calorie, low sodium, fruit and seafood specialities.

Expedite check-in   * Ask your travel agent to issue boarding passes with tickets. This will allow you to check baggage at the curb at major airports and proceed directly to your gate upon arrival at the airport.

AIRPORT PARKING

If you drive yourself to the airport, check ahead for parking rates and availability. Jot the location where you park to save time finding your car. Most major airports have short- and long-term parking lots and provide a free shuttle every few minutes. Long-term parking is always less expensive.

GROUND TRANSPORTATION

AIRPORT ARRIVAL: Call ahead to arrange for transportation from the airport to your destination. You will experience less stress if you know how to secure a taxi, limousine, train, or bus. Take phone numbers and confirmation numbers with you. Know if you will need cash or what credit cards are accepted.

RENTAL CAR: Reserve in advance. Shop various agencies for the best rate for the size car you need. RENTAL CARS MUST BE CHARGED ON A CREDIT CARD. Make sure you have available credit to avoid embarrassment. Know in advance where to go for your rental car upon arrival. Get a map of the area where you will be driving and outline the route to your destination. Inclement weather or darkness when you arrive, increases the frustration of trying to find your hotel with travel fatigue. Fill with gas before returning the car or you will be charged a high refill price. If you use express check-in, be sure you get a detailed receipt for your expense report.

RETURN TO AIRPORT: Plan for your return trip transportation before you leave home.

BALANCING ACT FOR TRAVELERS
(Continued)

HOTEL RESERVATIONS

When making a reservation, inquire about special rates for extending your stay over a weekend to include leisure activities, or include your family.

Inquire about amenities such as:
- Non smoking rooms
- Breakfast, newspaper included
- Pool, spa
- Health club, exercise room
- Clock in room
- Hair dryer, irons available
- Special floors for women or business people

Many hotels offer credit on airline frequent flyer programs, or their own frequent visitor offers—inquire and take advantage.

Take your confirmation number with you.

HOTEL SAFETY

Check-in: Never use your home address and phone number when registering. There are individuals who operate networks to alert colleagues your residence is vacant. Don't help them rob your home while you are away.

Escape: Observe the nearest exit as you enter your room. Count the number of doorways between your room and the nearest stairwell in case you have to feel your way down a smoke filled corridor. Check windows for escape routes and be sure they lock securely. Read the fire instructions in your room.

Security: When you leave your room hang the "Do Not Disturb" sign on the door, leave a light on, and the television on. A robber would prefer breaking into a room where it is obvious "no one is home." Never leave valuables in your room. This includes money, travelers checks, jewelry, furs, video camera, airlines tickets, etc. Use the hotel safe deposit box system.

Personal safety: While at the pool, spa, or exercise room, leave your room key at the front desk if the room number is on it. Anyone who observes your room number on your key will know your room is empty. Don't invite a robbery. When traveling alone, it is best not to invite new relationships to insure your personal safety.

74

BALANCING ACT FOR TRAVELERS
(Continued)

PACKING TIPS

• Check the weather at your destination before you pack.

• Select wardrobe color for the trip. If you try to mix color schemes for travel, it will require too many shoes, accessories, and basic items. Stay with the basic color for short trips.

• Assemble all items before packing.

• Use a checklist to avoid forgotten items.

CARRY-ON should include:

• Cash/travelers checks (take small bills for tipping)
• Credit cards/checkbook (carry a list of credit card numbers separate from your wallet)
• Medication
• Sunglasses
• Kleenex
• Airline ticket
• Frequent flyer cards
• Confirmation numbers for transportation and hotel
• Telephone credit card
• Map of destination area
• Business cards
• Reading material
• Luggage keys
• Stamps
• Cosmetics/change of underwear (basics if your luggage doesn't reach your destination for 24 hours)
• Umbrella
• Valuables
• Phone numbers

LUGGAGE

• Label inside and outside with business address
• Personal care items (pack only travel size shampoo, conditioner, toothpaste etc. Regular sizes weigh too much and are too bulky)
• Keep your travel kit of personal care items full and ready at all times. It reduces your packing time. Refill each time you return home as you unpack.
• Always take a small supply of first aid and emergency items in a zip-lock bag (bandaids, aspirin, safety pin, sewing items)
• Coordinate clothes to minimize the number of items and accessories you need.
• If you're inclined to shop while traveling, invest in a soft, collapsible piece of luggage. Pack it inside your regular luggage for bringing home treasures and bargains.
• A laundry bag helps to keep soiled clothes separate and expedites unpacking.
• Always lock your luggage.
• A study strap fastened around a suitcase will help you identify it easily and it will stay intact if the hinges or fastener should pop open.
• Pack spillables in a zip-lock bag in case the lid loosens during travel.

BALANCING ACT FOR THOSE WHO WORK EXTENDED HOURS

Many hard working individuals have expressed concern over being away from home during critical family time, missing social events, and generally becoming so career focused that home and leisure suffer.

As a key employee (such as a manager) you may be expected to attend to business beyond eight hours a day, travel on personal time, attend corporate events, dinners, or breakfast meetings.

If you can relate to any of the following symptoms, perhaps you will benefit from the tips other executives have passed on:

Symptom	Tips from experienced individuals
Only home during dark hours	Trade a late evening for an early morning Alternate working weekends for evenings Work at home when you can
Absence of fun activities on calendar	Find a friend to join you in some form of exercise once a week Schedule a fun activity for an afternoon, then go back to work
Spouse attends childrens' activities alone	Have a monthly family meeting to calendar childrens' activities. Book business around the events you want to attend Create a taped message to leave with your children to encourage them in their activities you miss Have spouse take photos. Relive the activity with your child through the photos
Feelings of extreme stress/guilt	Schedule a day off and take care of the cause Have an undistracted phone conversation with someone you love during the day Go home for lunch, do something you have been putting off even if it's just to begin a project
Falling behind in paying bills, buying groceries, laundry, cleaners, gardening, home repairs, washing/repairing car, visiting doctor/dentist	Keep a list of personal items you must attend to Designate 30 minutes of your day to personal business Hire help, and don't feel guilty

THE JOY OF RELOCATION

Here are some tips to help you retain your sanity during relocation—always a stressful but exciting time.

1. Keep a *notebook* with you at all times to jot down things you must do.

2. Open a *checking account* in your new city immediately so that you will have checks and available cash when you arrive. Use your new business address until you have a residence.

3. Finding your *new home* will take considerable time. You will need to take time off the job and your company will expect you to. Don't feel guilty about it. It's normal to feel discouraged after two or three excursions with a Realtor. When the place is right it will feel like home when you first walk in. Stay positive.

4. Establish your *move date* and work backwards to calendar things you must do.

5. Ask your moving company for a relocation *checklist* and timetable. They will provide you with everything you need to do, a step at a time.

THE JOY OF RELOCATION
(Continued)

One of the fastest way to unbalance your life is to accept an opportunity to transfer. It can also be one of the most positive steps you can take to improve the quality of life and promote your career. When the opportunity is presented to you it will surely cause you sleepless nights and endless pains of anxiety.

BEFORE YOU MAKE THE DECISION

Consider the work itself	What will be expected of you? Will it require extended hours? Is it work you enjoy? Will it be a learning experience? What authority, staff and budget will you have? How will you be compensated? Can it lead to greater opportunities?
Visit the new location	Meet people you will work with Inspect the physical environment Explore the city Make a list of the activities you enjoy, check for availability Read a local newspaper Identify things to do that are not available in your old location Visit the Chamber of Commerce, they can answer all questions
Before making the decision	Inspect your relocation package Clearly understand all policies List the benefits and consequences Weigh the differences Discuss it only with optimistic people Include your immediate family in the decision Don't discuss with people who may discourage you

You will feel less of a burden once you have made the decision. When you accept the offer, a clock begins ticking away the time you have left in your comfortable surroundings. A new anxiety will erupt within you. Suddenly there is more to do than you have time for and you may question if you are doing the right thing. It resembles "buyer's remorse." Enjoy the excitement of a new life. Look forward, not backwards. Without some pain and discomfort there can be no growth.

OUTSIDE EDUCATION

The desire to get ahead is a strong motivation. It is common for adults to take the initiative in setting new learning goals. More businesses now require specialized skills for employment and promotion. As technology advances the workforce must keep current. As we seek professional development we also develop new skills that enhance our personal lives.

Whether you desire an undergraduate degree, an MBA or PHD, a professional certificate or designation, or a new technical skill, making the decision to further your education will probably throw your life out of balance temporarily.

Some suggestions:

A. **SELECT THE RIGHT PROGRAM:** There are degree programs offered through the night or weekend classes, or independent study. There are programs for working professionals, extension programs, correspondence classes, and independent learning curriculums. Identify which kind of program is the easiest to integrate into your lifestyle. You will undoubtedly need to give up something you like doing to allow time for classes and study. Whatever you give up, use it as a reward when you complete a class or project.

B. **APPLY FOR CORPORATE ASSISTANCE:** Many companies reimburse tuition for employees. Find out if your company has a program and how to qualify. Some businesses allow time off the job for certification in skill building, job related areas.

C. **DON'T SET YOURSELF UP TO FAIL:** Be realistic when you enroll. Determine how much time you can commit each day or week and don't exceed it. It's better to take a year longer to finish, than to give up due to overload, or because the stress is killing you. Gain your family/friends support. They will help you stay focused on your goal and build in social activities that won't distract you if you are clearly committed and ask for their help.

D. **DESIGNATE STUDY TIME:** You should plan your study time, business hours, family time, and some social activities to keep a perspective on life while you further your education. Put your plan in writing and post it where you and your family/friends can see it. Exercise and mental breaks are essential. Reward yourself when you complete a paper, project or class. Take a long weekend away, buy yourself something, go out on the town, or sleep in. Celebrate before you take the next step, it helps you maintain some balance.

Decide what the education is that you want, why you want it, and then develop effective habits for self-improvement. To conquer an education goal and maintain a balance in your life is a big challenge. It will require dynamic organizational skills and planning ahead. Once committed, stick to it—there is always an end worth celebrating.

SUMMARY

> Balance is a do-it-yourself project. Many are able to balance home and career. Others struggle forever and jeopardize relationships, careers and happiness at home. Review this book as often as it takes for you to make progress in bringing balance into your life.

If you feel that you cannot achieve balance alone, call for professional help for guidance. To access an Employee Assistance Program you must work for a company that offers this type of program to their employees. You can locate a non-profit organization or independent professional by checking your telephone directory or by inquiring with United Way.

THE BEST BALANCE EXERCISE

Read the following questions and place a check in the appropriate column to see if you have developed an attitude that will make you a winner.

	Will Succeed In Balancing Home & Career	Will Not Be Able To Create A Good Balance
1. People who are organized and have a sense of priority	____	____
2. People who expect special consideration from the boss	____	____
3. People who feel guilty about their choice of career	____	____
4. People who have variety built into their lives	____	____
5. People who never have enough time	____	____
6. People who feel anxious and stressed	____	____
7. People who plan time wisely	____	____
8. People who have satisfied their basic need to belong and become involved	____	____
9. People who don't get enough exercise	____	____
10. People who are work-a-holics	____	____
11. People who eat whatever is the easiest when hungry	____	____
12. People who can define what they want in life	____	____
13. People who feel resentment toward responsibility	____	____
14. People who get enough exercise to relieve stress	____	____
15. People who are bored and lack motivation to change	____	____
16. People who use their energy to be productive	____	____
17. People who have a negative attitude towards change	____	____
18. People who plan meals, budgets, and outings	____	____
19. People who are afraid to try something new	____	____
20. People who are happy at home and happy in their career	____	____

(ANSWERS ON NEXT PAGE)

ANSWERS TO: THE BEST BALANCE EXERCISE

	Will Succeed In Balancing Home & Career	Will Not Be Able To Create A Good Balance
1. People who are organized and have a sense of priority	√	
2. People who expect special consideration from the boss		√
3. People who feel guilty about their choice of career		√
4. People who have variety built into their lives	√	
5. People who never have enough time		√
6. People who feel anxious and stressed		√
7. People who plan time wisely	√	
8. People who have satisfied their basic need to belong and become involved	√	
9. People who don't get enough exercise		√
10. People who are work-a-holics		√
11. People who eat whatever is the easiest when hungry		√
12. People who can define what they want in life	√	
13. People who feel resentment toward responsibility		√
14. People who get enough exercise to relieve stress	√	
15. People who are bored and lack motivation to change		√
16. People who use their energy to be productive	√	
17. People who have a negative attitude towards change		√
18. People who plan meals, budgets, and outings	√	
19. People who are afraid to try something new		√
20 People who are happy at home and happy in their career	√	

YOUR ACTION PLAN

$\boxed{\textbf{DO IT NOW}}$

You live with yourself longer than anyone else in the world. To help bring better balance into your life you need an action plan communicated to someone who will support you and can provide feedback on your progress. Isolation creates stress and pressure. Ask for help when you need it. There are Employee Assistance Programs and agencies waiting for your call. Refer to page 79 for ways to contact them.

Complete this plan of action. Then set up a meeting with a person you trust who will give you honest feedback.

AREAS WHERE I AM OUT OF BALANCE:

Home— _____

_____

Career— _____

_____

Leisure— _____

_____

THINGS I MUST <u>START</u> DOING	**THINGS I MUST <u>STOP</u> DOING**
Daily _____	Daily _____
_____	_____
Weekly _____	Weekly _____
_____	_____
Monthly _____	Monthly _____
_____	_____

PEOPLE I NEED TO COMMUNICATE WITH IN ORDER TO CREATE CHANGE IN MY:

Home— _____

Career— _____

Leisure— _____

TO: _____
         (name)

I am committed to creating a better balance between my home and my career. I agree to the steps I have outlined above and ask you to hold me accountable for them.

_____
Signed

*This agreement can be initiated by you, your spouse, your boss, a close friend, or relative. It's purpose is to motivate you to incorporate concepts and techniques of this program into your daily activities. It provides a gentle degree of accountability for you to take some positive action.

AUTHOR'S SOLUTIONS TO CASES

DEBBIE'S DILEMMA: It is the opinion of the author that Debbie's situation is not unique. Her feelings of guilt, resentment and anxiety have made her concentrate on the negative aspects of daily survival. The children can do more to contribute to household organization and family teamwork. Debbie's role in life is different than her mother's was when she was growing up and she may need to adjust her standards and expectations.

1. She ought to begin to network with other single parents who are comfortable with their lives.

2. Debbie and her children could spend a few minutes each evening getting ready for the morning take-off by preparing lunches, putting toys and coats by the door, etc. Breakfast can be simplified and even set on the table before bed.

3. She should learn to accept the children's performance in making their beds. Her standards are at the adult level.

4. A television rule is needed. TV only in the evening after homework will help.

5. Debbie may be able to plan time each day when she can give John 100% of her attention. His behavior at school and lack of enthusiasm in the morning could be an indication that John needs more balance in his life too.

6. Debbie could be more organized. Weekend meal planning and preparation will eliminate morning decisions. Cookies can be baked and frozen on weekends or purchased. Time for laundry and housecleaning can be planned and shared with the children. If there is a special event planned when the work is done, it will promote enthusiasm and teamwork.

7. One fun event each week could be planned. Debbie and the children need something to look forward to. Debbie also needs time just for herself.

8. There are some benefits to being single. Getting involved in a community activity can provide adult contact, bring some contrast to her life, and help her accept her role as a single parent.

THE MISSING RELATIONSHIP: The opinion of the author is that John is responsible for his own stress and should consider the following.

1. Set a goal to get on a regular exercise program. Commit to a one hour workout twice a week. Exercise provides a greater tolerance for stress.

2. John needs to examine his relationship with Joanne and decide if it is worth salvaging. If potential for a future together exists, then the relationship deserves as much energy and enthusiasm as John puts into his job.

3. Communicating with his boss on a regular basis is important. Keeping employees motivated and challenged is part of the boss' job. John should schedule a weekly meeting to communicate his department's accomplishments, and future plans.

4. John could target one weekend a month to get away, relax, and enjoy the outdoors.

5. Perhaps a close look at how he really spends his time on the job would enable John to better prioritize his activities.

THE BUSY COUPLE: The author feels that Mark and Mary are trying to juggle their lives individually instead of as a team.

1. Better communication is needed between Mark and Mary regarding their roles and responsibilities. Mary is trying to juggle too many time-consuming jobs. If Mark recognized the stress and frustration she is experiencing he would probably be willing to share the responsibilities of their home.

2. Mary should examine her priorities and determine if she really want to spend weekends on photographic excursions. If she does, then she and Mark may be willing to pay the price by doing weekend chores on weeknights together.

3. Examining the budget would reveal their ability to hire a house cleaning service. There might be something worth giving up to help relieve them of some housework or they may be willing to accept a different standard of living.

4. Cooking and planning ahead will build a reserve of meals in the freezer and eliminate the need for fast food. Exploring low-fat foods available through grocery stores and fast-food restaurants may help them reverse their weight gain.

5. Both could look for ways to lose weight and commit to regular exercise.

THE PARENT TRAP: The author's opinion is that Joe and Maria should examine their values together so that they communicate the same message to their children

1. As a runner, Joe has found a way to release or tolerate his stress. Maria has no stress outlet and could find some positive method of allowing it to escape.

2. Perhaps it would help if Joe and Maria re-examined their values and distribution of household and family responsibilities. They may feel that they have split them equally, however as life changes the reality may be that responsibilities need to change too.

3. Maria and Joe need time to communicate one to one. Allocating a special time each week will allow them to make contact with each other.

4. Parents are more effective when they maintain consistent standards when raising children. Sometimes parents need to confer before directing their children or allowing them privileges.

5. Perhaps a family outing once a month should be a priority. Ideas for outings could be considered from all family members and the events scheduled in advance so there is something to look forward to.

At the beginning of this program is was stated that this book would help you understand your challenges, determine opportunities you want to explore, and help establish the steps you need to take to balance your life.

Nobody can force you to make any changes. Only you can decide to act on suggestions provided in this book.

Take a moment to reflect on what you have read and then decide how to begin to activate your new action plan.

TO SUMMARIZE

- To achieve a better balance in your HOME you should keep the homefront positive. Define and communicate the goals and expectations you have about home, and then establish an action plan to insure they are accomplished.

- Your CAREER will grow when you meet the challenge of becoming a productive employee. The expectations of your job must be understood and agreed to. You need to develop a career action plan.

- Personal time should be allocated daily for LEISURE activities that provide fun, exercise and diversion from home and career. A monthly calendar will allow you to look forward to the events that become a necessary balancing element.

- CHILDREN offer another challenge to your balancing act. Home demands are greater when you have children. Your supervisor should maintain the same expectations from working parents as single people. Convenient, reliable child care is essential if parents are to achieve better balance. Building self-esteem in your children and training them to become more responsible will better prepare them to balance their own homes and careers when the time comes.

- Many of the tips and suggestions in this book might not be possible if your ability to cope is being challenged by physical or mental abuse, alcoholism, drug abuse or other dependency. Healthy families and individuals seek help. If you can't manage or accomplish change, PLEASE don't delay in finding help.

REMEMBER... No one can do it all. The objective is not to be a "superperson", simply to identify and take action on items which will bring better balance into your life. Any step toward balance is progress toward a happier life. Good luck!

GET RID OF
UNWANTED FEELINGS NOW

Negative feelings are often by-products of the daily struggle to keep our lives in balance. When these feelings build up, they undermine our confidence on the job and at home or take away from a good sense of well being. We must learn to get rid of unwanted negative feelings in order to balance the demands of home and work.

THE BLAME GAME

A GAME FOR ONE PLAYER.
START BY SELECTING YOUR LUCKY NUMBER BETWEEN
1 AND 7 AND MOVE FORWARD THAT MANY SPACES.

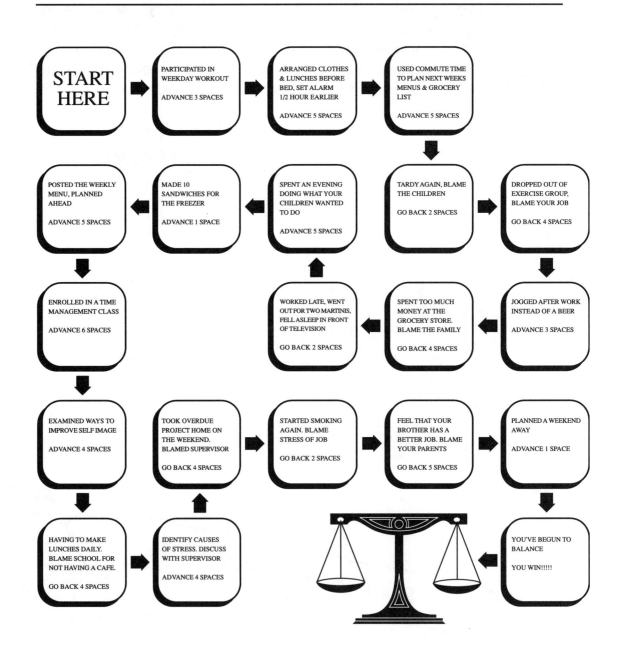

START HERE

PARTICIPATED IN WEEKDAY WORKOUT
ADVANCE 3 SPACES

ARRANGED CLOTHES & LUNCHES BEFORE BED, SET ALARM 1/2 HOUR EARLIER
ADVANCE 5 SPACES

USED COMMUTE TIME TO PLAN NEXT WEEKS MENUS & GROCERY LIST
ADVANCE 5 SPACES

POSTED THE WEEKLY MENU, PLANNED AHEAD
ADVANCE 5 SPACES

MADE 10 SANDWICHES FOR THE FREEZER
ADVANCE 1 SPACE

SPENT AN EVENING DOING WHAT YOUR CHILDREN WANTED TO DO
ADVANCE 5 SPACES

TARDY AGAIN, BLAME THE CHILDREN
GO BACK 2 SPACES

DROPPED OUT OF EXERCISE GROUP, BLAME YOUR JOB
GO BACK 4 SPACES

ENROLLED IN A TIME MANAGEMENT CLASS
ADVANCE 6 SPACES

WORKED LATE, WENT OUT FOR TWO MARTINIS, FELL ASLEEP IN FRONT OF TELEVISION
GO BACK 2 SPACES

SPENT TOO MUCH MONEY AT THE GROCERY STORE. BLAME THE FAMILY
GO BACK 4 SPACES

JOGGED AFTER WORK INSTEAD OF A BEER
ADVANCE 3 SPACES

EXAMINED WAYS TO IMPROVE SELF IMAGE
ADVANCE 4 SPACES

TOOK OVERDUE PROJECT HOME ON THE WEEKEND. BLAMED SUPERVISOR
GO BACK 4 SPACES

STARTED SMOKING AGAIN. BLAME STRESS OF JOB
GO BACK 2 SPACES

FEEL THAT YOUR BROTHER HAS A BETTER JOB. BLAME YOUR PARENTS
GO BACK 5 SPACES

PLANNED A WEEKEND AWAY
ADVANCE 1 SPACE

HAVING TO MAKE LUNCHES DAILY. BLAME SCHOOL FOR NOT HAVING A CAFE.
GO BACK 4 SPACES

IDENTIFY CAUSES OF STRESS. DISCUSS WITH SUPERVISOR
ADVANCE 4 SPACES

YOU'VE BEGUN TO BALANCE
YOU WIN!!!!!

NOW AVAILABLE FROM CRISP PUBLICATIONS

Books • Videos • CD Roms • Computer-Based Training Products

Subject Areas Include:

Management
Human Resources
Communication Skills
Personal Development
Marketing/Sales
Organizational Development
Customer Service/Quality
Computer Skills
Small Business and Entrepreneurship
Adult Literacy and Learning
Life Planning and Retirement

CRISP WORLDWIDE DISTRIBUTION

English language books are distributed worldwide. Major international
distributors include:

ASIA/PACIFIC

Australia/New Zealand: In Learning, PO Box 1051, Springwood QLD, Brisbane,
Australia 4127   Tel: 61-7-3-841-2286, Facsimile: 61-7-3-841-1580
ATTN: Messrs. Gordon

Singapore: 85, Genting Lane, Guan Hua Warehouse Bldng #05-01, Singapore
349569   Tel: 65-749-3389, Facsimile: 65-749-1129
ATTN: Evelyn Lee

Japan: Phoenix Associates Co., LTD., Mizuho Bldng. 3-F, 2-12-2, Kami Osaki,
Shinagawa-Ku, Tokyo 141   Tel: 81-33-443-7231, Facsimile: 81-33-443-7640
ATTN: Mr. Peter Owans

CANADA

Reid Publishing, Ltd., Box 69559-109 Thomas Street, Oakville, Ontario
Canada L6J 7R4.   Tel: (905) 842-4428, Facsimile: (905) 842-9327
ATTN: Mr. Stanley Reid

Trade Book Stores: *Raincoast Books,* 8680 Cambie Street, Vancouver, B.C.,
V6P 6M9   Tel: (604) 323-7100, Facsimile: (604) 323-2600
ATTN: Order Desk

EUROPEAN UNION

England: *Flex Training,* Ltd. 9-15 Hitchin Street, Baldock, Hertfordshire,
SG7 6A, England   Tel: 44-1-46-289-6000, Facsimile: 44-1-46-289-2417
ATTN: Mr. David Willetts

INDIA

Multi-Media HRD, Pvt., Ltd., National House, Tulloch Road, Appolo Bunder,
Bombay, India 400-039   Tel: 91-22-204-2281, Facsimile: 91-22-283-6478
ATTN: Messrs. Aggarwal

SOUTH AMERICA

Mexico: *Grupo Editorial Iberoamerica,* Nebraska 199, Col. Napoles, 03810
Mexico, D.F.   Tel: 525-523-0994, Facsimile: 525-543-1173
ATTN: Señor Nicholas Grepe

SOUTH AFRICA

Alternative Books, Unit A3 Micro Industrial Park, Hammer Avenue, Stridom Park,
Randburg, 2194 South Africa   Tel: 27-11-792-7730, Facsimile: 27-11-792-7787
ATTN: Mr. Vernon de Haas